With his extensive experience and understanding, David Holloway has reflected deeply on the Church of England. We at Latimer, in partnership with Renew, offer this booklet to encourage further reflection. In keeping with its original form as an address to the staff team at St Helen's Bishopsgate, referencing has been kept to a minimum.

Renew 2022

THE ENGLISH REFORMED TRADITION:

ITS DISTINCTIVES

AND WORTH

DAVID HOLLOWAY

The Latimer Trust

CONTENTS

Introduction	I
My Own Journey	2
The Classic Answer	3
The Lutheran tradition	6
The Calvinistic tradition	7
Reformed Catholicism	8
Anglican Moderation	10
Anglican Differences and Distinctives	12
Regulative Principle	14
On the Doctrine of the Church	16
On the Papacy	20
Severe Logic and Predestination	23
The Problem of Lowest Common Denominator Theology	31
On Marriage and Sex	35
Appendix: The Reform Covenant	41

Introduction

The content of this study, *The English Reformed Tradition: Its Distinctives and Worth,* began as a Zoom lecture to the staff of St Helen's Bishopsgate and its associated churches during the first Covid lockdown in 2020. William Taylor, the rector, suggested it had a wider audience, hence this publication. It is written in response to the twenty-first-century doctrinal and ethical confusion in the Anglican tradition generally and the Church of England in particular. And it is written with the conviction that, first, you face the confusion as a hard fact and reality. However, secondly, it is written with the English Reformed instinct that you follow the Apostolic ecclesiology expressed by John in Revelation 2–3 and the letters to seven churches in the Roman Province of Asia. So you are not surprised when churches and clergy fail: on the one hand, when they fail in terms of Christian doctrine or ethics (like the Churches in Pergamum and Thyatira); or, on the other hand, when they fail in terms of practical love of God and neighbour (like the 'sound' church, the Church in Ephesus). But we are to note this: the churches were treated as seven individual churches, but, institutionally, as one in chapters 2–3. For John was instructed to write the seven letters in *one* book. Also 'the seven stars [which] are the angels of seven churches' are in *one* hand, 'the right hand' of the risen Jesus. So, with that said, how should we respond to our confused state? Surely, as John did, by not suggesting schism but working for robust repentance and where necessary discipline.

My Own Journey

Tertullian, the early Latin Church Father, at the end of the second century, issued a warning. It was a warning against listening to any theological discussion unless you know the spiritual pedigree of the writer. He said:

> We admit no man to any disputation concerning sacred things, or to the scanning and examining of particular questions of religion, unless he first show us of whom he received the faith, by whose means he became a Christian, and whether he admit and hold the general principles wherein all Christians do, and ever did, agree.

So first I will say something of my own pilgrimage and pedigree. The key influences on me which are relevant to this topic were in the late 1950s and early 60s. First, in my university vacations, there was a North London evangelical rector, while in term-time there was the Christian Union with men like the young John Stott, the young Jim Packer, and the young Michael Green being regular visitors.

Secondly, there was Basil Gough, the Rector of St Ebbe's Church in Oxford, and his confirmation classes – which were basically on the Thirty-Nine Articles and the *Book of Common Prayer*.

Thirdly, there was an unknown clergyman, dressed in a cassock and dog-collar, standing on the chancel steps of St Ebbe's, giving consecutive addresses for the Christian Union mission. This was the first systematic and coherent exposition of the Christian faith I had ever heard. The unknown clergyman, went by the name of Richard Lucas.

With that said, I must address what Tertullian would call the 'theological question' we are considering, namely: What is the English Reformed tradition? How does it differ from other Reformed traditions? And why is it worth preserving?

The Classic Answer

The classic answer has to begin with Sir Thomas Browne. He was a seventeenth-century medical doctor, who wrote about the Church of England at the time of the Reformation. In his *Religio Medici,* published in 1642, he said this:

> As there were many Reformers, so likewise many Reformations; every Country proceeding in a particular way and method, according as their national Interest, together with their Constitution and Clime, inclined them.[1]

---

[1] Sir Thomas Browne, *Religio Medici* (1642), https://ccel.org/ccel/browne/religio/religio.ii.i.html

3

He then gave high praise to the Church of England 'whose Articles, Constitutions and Customs seem so consonant unto reason'. He also referred to Luther, Calvin, the Council of Trent, and the Synod of Dort. So we have to realise that there were various Reformed traditions.

Five were alluded to by Thomas Browne – the Saxon tradition of Luther, the Genevan tradition of Calvin, the Dutch tradition at Dort, Rome (trying to reform itself) – and, yes, the English tradition of the Church of England as Elizabeth I had left it. Browne was writing his book with King Charles I still (just) on the throne. And the Puritan-majority Westminster Assembly, wanting to restructure the Church of England, began just after Browne had finished the first edition of his book. The Civil War had started in 1642. It was a frenzied situation. But Browne did not want the destruction of the Church of England. And he wrote about things not covered by the Thirty-Nine Articles and the *Book of Common Prayer* – the 'standards' for what became the mainstream English Reformed tradition – as follows:

> Whatsoever is beyond, as points indifferent, I observe according to the rules of my private reason, or the humour and fashion of my Devotion; neither believing this, because Luther affirmed it, or disproving that, because Calvin hath disavouched it. I condemn not all things in the Council of Trent, nor approve all in the Synod of Dort.

> In brief, where the Scripture is silent,
> the Church is my Text; where, that [the
> Church] speaks, 'tis but my Comment;
> where there is joynt silence of both, I
> borrow not the rules of my Religion from
> Rome or Geneva, but the dictates of my
> own reason.

That is the classic method of the English Reformed
tradition as seen by a layman – Scripture, first and
absolute; then, the tradition of the church (the wisdom of
the Christian centuries and contemporaries that agree);
then, my own view or reason. But you have to be careful
about this word 'tradition' and how you define it. Yes, you
can read the key results of the Council of Trent and, today,
the current Church of Rome's tradition in its Catechism
of the Catholic Church – popular and definitive 2000
edition, 778 pages long.

It is relatively easy to define the English Reformed
tradition because its historic doctrinal defining
documents have been few and they have been enshrined
in the law of the land. So these legally, define uniquely
and simply, the Church of England. For now, a Church of
England Measure has the force of an Act of Parliament –
it is a statute.

And, so, the English tradition (as Reformed) has been
Established; and, with the monarch as the supreme
layperson, it is defined legally in the Church of England

(Worship and Doctrine) Measure 1974 in words that also form the Church of England's Canon A5:

> The doctrine of the Church of England is grounded in the Holy Scriptures, and in such teachings of the ancient Fathers and Councils of the Church as are agreeable to the said Scriptures. In particular such doctrine is to be found in the Thirty-Nine Articles of Religion, *The Book of Common Prayer*, and the Ordinal.

In passing, that implies at least the clauses that make up the Reform Covenant, a copy of which is in an appendix, and assent to which is being required by an increasing number of Anglican committees and leadership teams. For it is a good definition of the English Reformed tradition.

The Lutheran Tradition

However, for the Lutheran tradition you have to go to its *Book of Concord* of 1580 with a great number of texts forming its doctrinal basis: the three Creeds; the Augsburg Confession of 1530; the Apology of the Augsburg Confession (a vast document) of 1531; the Smalcald Articles of Luther (1537); the Treatise on the Power of the Pope (1537); the Small Catechism of Luther (1529), the Large Catechism of Luther (1529), the Epitome of the Formula of Concord (1577) and The Solid or Thorough Declaration of the Formula of Concord (1577).

The Calvinistic Tradition

But, if you ask, 'What is the Calvinistic tradition?', where do you start? There are so many traditions in different countries. Take America. In the USA, there are a dozen Reformed denominations and perhaps another half a dozen with a Reformed heritage.

And by the way, this is one reason why I am not advising people to leave the Church of England. It was disastrous in 1662. The Calvinistic Congregationalist Pilgrim Fathers had already left, of course. But splits in this Calvinistic Puritan tradition have given rise to so many further splits, about which Thomas Browne, again, was quite perceptive:

> Heads that are disposed unto Schism and complexionally propense [inclined by temperament] to innovation, are naturally indisposed for a community, nor will be ever confined unto the order or economy of one body; and therefore, when they separate from others, they knit but loosely among themselves; nor contented with a general breach or dichotomy with their Church do subdivide and mince themselves almost into Atoms.

However, back to the Calvinist tradition. Calvin, the progenitor of the tradition, like Luther, wrote so much (or had written for him by way of transcription). And his thinking was necessarily developing – witness the

7

number of editions of his *Institutes of the Christian Religion*. So where is a clear statement of this tradition?

Answer: fortunately, it is in the publicly agreed and published documents of the Westminster Assembly that met and worked in London from 1643 to 1653. These, in addition to the Westminster Confession, include the Larger and Shorter Catechisms, the Directory of Public Worship, and Presbyterial Church Government. All were adopted by the Scottish Church and Government but not all the paragraphs of the Confession by the English Government at that time (as we shall see), and with the Act of Uniformity of 1662, and the imposition of the *Book of Common Prayer*, the Confession was rejected as law.

However, in spite of the English reserve over some of the Westminster Confession, because of its merits it became influential throughout the English-speaking world, and especially in America. So, these documents were – and often still are – representative of the wider non-Anglican Reformed tradition. Therefore, it is fair to treat these as the Calvinistic interpretation of the Christian faith in contrast to the mainstream English Reformed tradition which is Anglican. So, we will proceed on that basis.

Reformed Catholicism

One more important point before we get down to the key distinctives of the English Reformed tradition. As our friend Thomas Browne said on the history of our English Reformed tradition: 'It is an unjust scandal of our adversaries, and a gross error in our selves, to compute the

8

Nativity of our Religion from Henry the Eighth.' Browne was making the obvious point that what was being reformed was something *already in existence* – namely 'the church of Christ truly catholic'. In other words, it was a reform of God's church as a whole ('catholic' being the transliteration of the Greek for the Latin 'universal').

All the magisterial Reformers (ie those involved with the State) wanted to be 'catholic' Christians – unlike some of the radical Reformers like the Anabaptists (many of whom were far more extreme than Baptists today, of course). But gradually the word 'catholic' from its use in the phrase 'catholic creeds and councils', importantly came to imply *doctrinal* universality and not just *territorial* universality which the word 'universal' can imply. And, practically, in their 'catholicity', these Reformers claimed to be going back to the wisdom of the early Fathers of the church (and they were) – and not just to the New Testament, as it were, nakedly. But these early Fathers pointed them back to the Scriptures. So it was a Scriptural Catholicity. In the Anglican Homilies in *An Exhortation to Obedience*, there is reference to 'the Catholic faith contained in Holy Scripture.'[2] So our English tradition is truly *catholic* but it is *reformed* catholic.

---

[2] *Certain Homilies or Sermons appointed to be read in Churches in the time of Queen Elizabeth,* http://www.anglicanlibrary.org/homilies/

Anglican Moderation

Our tradition is not a 'halfway house'. It is unhelpful to say that the Church of England is halfway between the Pope and Calvin. It is more correct to call it 'moderate'. It is a moderate Calvinistic church. But still be careful. Oliver O'Donovan rightly criticises the claim that 'Anglican moderation' is 'steering a steady middle path between the exaggerated positions of Rome on the one hand and Geneva on the other.' He says:

> There was nothing particularly 'middle' about most of the English Reformers' theological positions ... Their moderation consisted rather in a determined policy of separating the essentials of faith and order from *adiaphora* [things indifferent] ... Anglican moderation is the policy of reserving strong statement and conviction for the few things which really deserve them.[3]

The Anglican Settlement of Elizabeth I was by no means a fudge over essential matters. For from now on, the Church of England was theologically rooted in the Thirty-nine Articles, the *Prayer Book* and the Ordinal, along with the Homilies which were printed sermons to be read in churches. The first five sermons in the first

[3] Oliver O'Donovan, *On the Thirty-Nine Articles: A Conversation with Tudor Christianity* (Exeter: Paternoster, 1986), 14.

All the magisterial
Reformers wanted
to be 'catholic'
Christians. Our
English tradition is
truly catholic but it is
reformed catholic.

book of Homilies (written by Cranmer under Edward VI) are basic reading for the theology of the Church of England. They are on Scripture, Sin, Salvation, Faith and Good Works. They are still easy to read and they give you, in a short space, the gospel foundations of the Church of England. The second book of Homilies, published by the authority of Queen Elizabeth I, and more Puritan, is important in showing the concerns current at the time of the Settlement. When read in context, they are still relevant for today.

Anglican Differences and Distinctives

So now for some specific differences and distinctives.

How did these work out in practice? The Anglican Settlement of Elizabeth I certainly meant clearer distinctions between the English Reformed tradition enshrined in law and Roman Catholics – but it also led to distinctions with the other Reformed traditions. This accounts for how Anglicans can differ today from some of their Free Church friends. It is essential to understand the reasons for these differences. However, it all started with robes!

In 1565, with the Settlement more or less established, Queen Elizabeth wrote to her Archbishop at the time, Matthew Parker, saying she was not happy about the way clergy were failing to robe in services. They were not conforming to the *Prayer Book* which, after all, was a Protestant and not a Roman Catholic book, and she herself had championed it. Parker tried to take the side of the clergy along with other bishops. But their Reformed friends in Zurich, with whom some had taken refuge during Mary's reign of terror, advised the bishops and clergy to obey the Queen. What she was requiring, they said, was not a gospel issue.

Unfortunately, this issue had the effect of helping to divide biblical Protestants into conformist and non-conformist groups. The first non-conforming manifesto was entitled *A Brief Discourse against the Outward Apparel* (1566). It argued that, in themselves, vestments were harmless – but because they were associated with Rome, simple people could be led astray. A defence of conforming to the Anglican Settlement was given then by Archbishop Grindal, who succeeded Matthew Parker as Archbishop of Canterbury. He wrote to Henry Bullinger, who succeeded the Reformer Zwingli in Zurich thus:

> We who are bishops on our first return [after Mary], and before we entered on our ministry, contended long and earnestly for the removal of those things that have occasioned ... dispute; but as we were unable to prevail, either with the Queen or the Parliament, we judged it best, after consultation on the subject, not to desert our churches for the sake of a few ceremonies, and those not unlawful in themselves, especially since the pure

> doctrine of the gospel remained in all its
> integrity and freedom.

However, none of this was actually new. Elizabeth I was just following Cranmer and Ridley. In their day, John Hooper had been against robes. Cranmer would have none of it. A principle was at stake.

Regulative Principle

So Cranmer refused to consecrate Hooper until he changed his mind. Hooper's views were expressed in his *The Regulative Principle and Things Indifferent*:

> Nothing should be used in the Church which has not either the express Word of God to support it, or otherwise is a thing indifferent in itself which brings no profit when done or used, but no harm when not done or omitted.

That seemed fine. But then Hooper said – and this is important:

> Indifferent things must have their origin and foundation in the Word of God.

This is the Regulative Principle. It seems to mean that because robes (and wedding rings, together with a host of other things) are not mentioned in the New Testament, they cannot claim to have their origin in the Word of God. Therefore, it was argued, they ought to be ruled out. A response to Hooper's position was then given by Bishop

Ridley (later to be martyred under Queen Mary – as was Hooper himself). However, in 1551, Hooper conformed and became the Bishop of Gloucester. But he was, and still is, known as 'the father of English non-conformity'. Things were not really resolved, as is evident from what happened subsequently under Elizabeth and Archbishop Matthew Parker.

In some quarters, the issue is still alive today. And with the current leadership in modern institutionalised Anglicanism too often giving little evidence of a commitment to the English Reformed tradition, more seem to be moving to this non-conforming 'Puritan' tradition that has an instinct for the Regulative Principle where practices are not permitted unless clearly endorsed by the New Testament. This principle indicates a fundamental difference between the Anglican tradition and the non-conforming Westminster Confession of 1643. Chapter 21, section 1, says:

> ... the acceptable way of worshiping the true God is instituted by himself, and so limited by his own revealed will, that he may not be worshipped ... according to any way not prescribed in the Holy Scripture.

Some may already be asking, 'Isn't this all academic?' The answer has to be 'No!' For there is much to be said in favour of modest robes, festivals and the church's liturgical year, for example. Hooker said wisely, 'that the church is a society and a society supernatural'. Hence, we have to take note of how human societies work. For the church is not immune to the dysfunctions of human societies that robes, festivals and routines seek to address. To over-spiritualise the church and to ignore sociological realities is simply too other-worldly. However, very serious is the fact that this tradition rejects the Creeds! There is nothing in the Westminster Confession (or in the Directory of Public Worship) about Creeds. And evangelical free churches I visit still never recite the Creeds. That goes back to the 1640s and the Westminster Assembly.

On the Doctrine of the Church

All that leads us on to the doctrine of the church which the Church of England, I believe, has particularly got right. I refer to Article 19 of The Thirty-nine Articles entitled 'Of the Church', which says:

> The visible Church of Christ is a congregation of faithful men, in the which the pure Word of God is preached, and the Sacraments be duly ministered according to Christ's ordinance in all those things that of necessity are requisite to the same.

> As the Church of Jerusalem, Alexandria, and Antioch have erred; so also the Church of Rome hath erred, not only in their living and manner of Ceremonies, but also in matters of Faith.

The background then, as now, to this Article is that the Reformed churches, and the Reformed in the churches, did not really come to a common mind either in terms of the church's essence, its basic structure, or its relationship to the State. Indeed, there were deep disagreements. And there still are! But, surely Hooker identified the problem:

> For lack of diligent observing the difference, first between the Church of God mystical and visible, then between the visible sound and corrupted, sometimes more sometimes less, the oversights are neither few nor light that have been committed.

However, we have got what we have got and our Article is pretty clear. It is an attempt to state what is essential to being a church of Christ. Cranmer was following Luther in the Augsburg Confession in attempting to define the essence of the church. But, unlike Luther, he has the wisdom to define what 'church' he was talking about. It is the 'visible' church as distinct from the church 'mystical' (his term and a better term than 'invisible', as many of that church 'mystical' who are alive are, obviously, in the 'visible' church).

A substantive issue relates to what the word 'congregation' means in Article 19. This is still important for today. I once heard a bishop say it means the diocese not the local congregation. But that is not what the Article says. Article 19 defines 'the visible church' as 'a congregation' – note the indefinite 'a' – a local congregation. For where 'the pure Word of God is preached, and the Sacraments be duly ministered' visibly is not in the diocese (a geographical region) but in the fellowship of the local church, in my case Jesmond Parish Church. And arguing in this way is simply to follow the Royal Declaration that prefaces the Articles by saying a man

> ... shall submit to it [the text of the Articles] in the plain and full meaning thereof: and shall not put his own sense or comment to be the meaning of the Article, but shall take it in the literal and grammatical sense.

But what about the Lutherans if Cranmer was following Luther? Well, Luther's Augsburg Article 8 entitled 'What the Church is', simply says, 'The Church properly is the congregation of saints and true believers.'

That is the entire definition. So that looks like the church that is the church 'mystical' – because it is made up of 'true believers'. But Augsburg Article 8 then, confusingly, goes on to talk about the unworthiness of ministers which is covered in our Article 26. So, it cannot only be made up of true believers. It must be the church visible.

Practically, Luther acted with the local church as the congregation where sometimes the buck had to stop. For we find him writing to villagers of Leisnig in Saxony as follows:

> Wherever there is a Christian congregation in possession of the gospel, it not only has the right and power but also the duty – on pain of losing the salvation of its souls and in accordance with the promise made to Christ in baptism – to avoid, to flee, to depose, and to withdraw from the authority that our bishops ... and the like are now exercising.

That is the village church and not the diocese. That advice follows (in terms of catholicity) Augustine, who wrote:

> We should not obey those bishops who have been duly elected, if they commit errors, or teach or ordain anything contrary to the divine Scripture.

And that principle, without being directed to any particular body appears, in Augsburg Article 28, 'Of Ecclesiastical Power', the last Article of the entire Confession.

But what about the Calvinistic Westminster Confession? Well, Chapter 25 starts off with, 'the Catholic or universal church which is invisible' as the primary unit. It conspicuously does not use the word 'congregation'. Its primary focus is the church mystical, subordinate to which is the local church, of course. True, at the beginning of the sixteenth century, the Latin '*congregatio*' and the English 'congregation' could refer either to 'the whole body of the faithful' or a society of believers (like a diocese) or to a particular local assembly. So, you have to look at its context for the meaning. And interestingly, in our Article 19, Cranmer doesn't use the Latin word *congregatio* but *coetus* (a coming together).

So the English Reformed doctrine of the church is complex but clear enough. In outline our Reformers distinguished the church visible from the church 'mystical'; the church as a clerical institution from the church as people; and the national church from the local congregation. We could do worse than follow those distinctions. And let Hooker have the last word. He said that for 'convenience', churches like 'the Church of Jerusalem, Alexandria and Antioch' of Article 19 have to be 'limited' into 'several congregations termed parishes'.

On the Papacy

Let me now deal with some other fundamental issues which the Church of England, particularly has got right. First, a short comment on the Papacy.

The English Reformers held that the canonical Scripture – the Bible – was to be the supreme theological authority in the Church. That is why they were opposed to a Pope getting in the way of God and the believer. However, the English Reformed tradition came to be against all 'popes'. They were against the wrong sort of adulation for heroes among Protestants, as well as adulation for the Pope. Bishop J C Ryle, the first Anglican bishop of Liverpool, was a later strong exponent of this conviction. In his paper *The Fallibility of Ministers*, Ryle is arguing

The English Reformed
tradition came to be
against all 'popes'.
They were against
the wrong sort of
adulation for heroes
among Protestants.

that the church's Bible is the only infallible authority. That contrasts with the potential fallibility of all the church's ministers including the Reformers. After discussing the apostle Paul's public opposition to Peter at Antioch, recorded in Galatians 2:11–16, Ryle surveys some history and says:

> The first great lesson we learn from Antioch is that great ministers may make great mistakes. The Reformers were honoured instruments in the hand of God for reviving the cause of truth on earth. Yet hardly one of them can be named who did not make some great mistake. Martin Luther held pertinaciously the doctrine of consubstantiation. Melanchthon was often timid and undecided. Calvin permitted Servetus to be burned. Cranmer recanted and fell away for a time from his first faith. Jewel subscribed to Popish doctrine for fear of death. The Puritans, in after times, denounced toleration ... [and] Wesley and Toplady abused each other in the strongest language.[4]

This conviction is very releasing. For when a great teacher is wrong over something, it does not mean you reject all the good that teacher also teaches or has taught. No one is perfect!

---

[4] J C Ryle, 'The Fallibility of Ministers', *Knots Untied* (1874).

Only the Bible, says Ryle, is to be considered infallible (or to use Wycliffe's excellent and better term, 'incorrigible' – it cannot be corrected). And Hooker was concerned at the way some people were already putting Calvin in the place of Scripture and making him their 'pope'. They were reading him rather than the Bible. 'His books' were, says Hooker, 'almost the very canon to judge both doctrine and discipline by.' Hooker had a great respect for Calvin. But Hooker typifies the Anglican Reformed view. It is against any saying, in the brilliant words of Bob Fyall, the Old Testament scholar (and himself a Scottish Presbyterian): 'It is a pity Calvin didn't write the Bible'.

So first the papacy.

Severe Logic and Predestination

Secondly, comes what I call the 'severe logic' in some of the Westminster tradition and some other Reformed traditions, which the Anglican tradition avoids.

That is seen most clearly in the issue of predestination. Apart from the Regulative Principle, this was another main contention of our Anglican Reformers against some forms of Calvinism. And this Anglican position was not a compromise of Elizabeth I. It too was all there with Cranmer. Take Article 17 and compare that with the Westminster Confession, Chapter 3 entitled 'Of God's Eternal Decree'. In that chapter of the Westminster Confession we read this in section 5:

> Those of mankind that are predestined
> unto life, God, before the foundation
> of the world was laid, according to his
> eternal and immutable purpose, and
> the secret counsel and good pleasure
> of his will, hath chosen in Christ unto
> everlasting glory, out of his mere free
> grace and love, without any foresight of
> faith or good works, or perseverance in
> either of them, or any other thing in the
> creature, as conditions or causes moving
> him thereunto; and all to the praise of his
> glorious grace.

So, there is no foreseeing by God of who would believe
and then predestining them. No! It is all of God's 'secret
counsel and good pleasure'. This was not controversial.
The English Reformers agreed, as did the Roman
Catholic tradition. But then in section 7 of Chapter 3 of
the Westminster Confession, we read this:

> The rest of mankind, God was pleased,
> according to the unsearchable counsel
> of his own will, whereby he extendeth
> or withholdeth mercy as he pleaseth, for
> the glory of his sovereign power over his
> creatures, to pass by, and to ordain them
> to dishonour and wrath for their sin, to
> the praise of his glorious justice.

This is called 'reprobation' – the predestining of people to death and hell. But our English Reformers do not affirm this doctrine in our Articles. Here is Article 17 – it is entitled, 'Of Predestination and Election':

> Predestination to Life is the everlasting purpose of God, whereby (before the foundations of the world were laid) he hath constantly decreed by his counsel secret to us, to deliver from curse and damnation those whom he hath chosen in Christ to everlasting salvation, as vessels made to honour...

The Article goes on:

> As the godly consideration of Predestination, and our Election in Christ, is full of sweet, pleasant, and unspeakable comfort to godly persons ... So, for curious and carnal persons, lacking the Spirit of Christ, to have continually before their eyes the sentence of God's Predestination, is a most dangerous downfall, whereby the Devil doth thrust them either into desperation, or into wretchlessness of most unclean living, no less perilous than desperation.

> Furthermore, we must receive God's promises in such wise, as they be generally set forth to us in holy Scripture:

> and, in our doings, that Will of God is
> to be followed, which we have expressly
> declared unto us in the Word of God.

Our English Reformers realised that you had to be very
careful with the doctrine of predestination. Pastorally, if
presented wrongly, it could do more harm than good.
That is why they were so keen to keep the balance and
proportion of Scripture. So, they said: 'we must receive
God's promises in such wise, as they be generally set
forth to us in holy Scripture.'

We are to focus on obedience to God's clear will 'which
we have expressly declared unto us in the Word of God'.
We are not to waste time on speculation into God's
'counsel that is secret to us'. Our Reformers had looked
at the Bible and they found they should not jump to
conclusions about God's 'hidden wisdom'. And they
wanted biblical balance and proportion.

Because, first, the Bible shows that Jesus avoided talking
about 'double predestination'. In the Parable of the Sheep
and the Goats he speaks of the faithful believers who are
'blessed by my Father' (Matt 25:34) as inheriting 'the
kingdom prepared for you since the creation of the world'.
But with regard to the unfaithful – who are 'you who are
cursed' (25:41), yet with no mention of 'my Father' as the
curser – he speaks of 'eternal fire prepared [not for you]
but for the devil and his angels.'

Secondly, in Romans 9, where verses 14 and following
form a key passage on predestination, Paul says:

Our Reformers had
looked at the Bible and
they found they should
not jump to conclusions
about God's 'hidden
wisdom'. And they
wanted biblical balance
and proportion.

> What if God, although choosing to show his wrath and make his power known, bore with great patience the objects of his wrath – prepared for destruction? What if he did this to make the riches of his glory known to the objects of his mercy, whom he prepared in advance for glory (Rom 9:22–23).

Note the 'what if' – Paul hesitates about being dogmatic. Note also that God's sovereignty in this section is clearly a sovereignty of mercy. God is withholding immediate judgment: 'What if God ... bore with great patience the objects of wrath.' And note that Paul explicitly mentions in verse 23, 'objects of his mercy whom he [God] prepared in advance for glory', while in verse 22 Paul does not mention God as the agent. Paul referred simply to 'objects of wrath prepared for destruction' – not 'prepared by God for destruction'. It is a simple passive. No agent is mentioned.

Then, thirdly, in addition to Jesus and Paul, there is Peter who says in his first letter: 'They stumble because they disobey the message – which is also what they were destined for' (1 Pet 2:8). Again there is no agent. Peter does not say their disobedience was 'destined for by God'. Now, of course, logically if God is sovereign over all, logic says there must be a double predestination. But Jesus and the apostles did not teach this. They did not deny it. They kept silent.

There is a legitimate place for mystery or for us simply not to know. This side of heaven not everything is revealed, either by special revelation in Scripture or by general revelation through the natural order – as Psalm 19:1 teaches some things can be. But sufficient is revealed. Paul makes this clear:

> Now we see only a reflection as in a mirror; then we shall see face to face. Now I know in part: then I shall know fully, even as I am fully known (1 Cor 13:12).

Our Anglican forefathers were conscious of the Old Testament truth taught in Deuteronomy:

> The secret things belong to the Lord our God, but the things revealed belong to us and to our children forever, that we may follow all the words of this law (Deut 29:29).

Unlike some other Reformers, the Anglican Reformers were less 'systematic'. They did not write great theologies. They gave us instead Thirty-nine Articles and Homilies – serious sermons – not a Westminster Confession which is a mini systematic theology and, indeed, has much to teach us.

As Griffith Thomas, a former Principal of Wycliffe Hall, Oxford, put it:

There is obvious danger in every attempt at systematising Christian truth ... it is far better to be content with 'Articles' or 'points' with gaps unfilled ... This method prevents teaching becoming hardened into a cast iron system which cannot expand. It is the virtue of the Church of England articles that they ... do not commit Churchmen to an absolute, rigid system of doctrine.[5]

Bishop J C Ryle saw this 'over-systematising' also behind the concept of a 'limited' atonement where some Reformers asserted that Christ died only for 'the elect', not 'the world'. When commenting on John the Baptist's statement in John 1:29 that Jesus is the 'Lamb of God who takes away the sin of the world' and those who claim that this does not mean the world but the elect, Ryle writes this:

I hold as strongly as anyone that Christ's death is profitable to none but to the elect who believe in his name. But I dare not limit and pare down such expressions as the one before us. I dare not say that no atonement has been made in any sense, except for the elect. I believe it is possible to be more systematic than the Bible in

---

[5] W H Griffith Thomas, Preface to *The Principles of Theology: An Introduction to the Thirty-nine Articles* (London: Vine, 1978), 3.

our statements. When I read that the wicked who are lost, 'deny the Lord that bought them' (2 Pet 2:1) and that 'God was in Christ, reconciling the world unto himself' (2 Cor 5:19), I dare not confine the intentions of redemption to the saints alone. Christ is for every man.[6]

This seems to be the view of Cranmer too. In Article 31 we are told:

The offering of Christ once made is that perfect redemption, propitiation, and satisfaction for all the sins of the whole world, both original and actual; and there is none other satisfaction for sin, but that alone.

How, in the divine economy, Christ died 'for every man' surely remains one of those 'secret things that belong to the Lord our God.'

The Problem of Lowest Common Denominator Theology

As I draw to a close, let me mark one other way, among a number of others, why the English Reformed tradition is worth preserving. But first, a problem with our own tradition that we must deal with.

George Marsden, the US historian, studied the traditions of those 20 US Reformed (or with Reformed heritage)

---

[6] J C Ryle, *Expository Thoughts in the Gospels: John vol 1*, 61–62.

denominations and groups. He saw three identities. First, the doctrinalists – sticklers for the Westminster Assembly. Secondly, the Dutch tradition from Dort via Abraham Kuyper and, in the modern age, Francis Schaeffer – with their concern for the whole of the culture and Christ's Lordship over all of life. And, thirdly, the tradition of mainstream American evangelicalism, from places like Trinity Evangelical Divinity School, Fuller Seminary, the Billy Graham Organization, the Gospel Coalition, and in England, of course, the Proclamation Trust, the Christian Institute, and UCCF – in fact, many of us, English Reformed people. But the history of such evangelicalism is that, necessarily because of their distinctives, they have a lowest common denominator theology. That Marsden says is from:

> ... the evangelical-pietist tradition – a certain style of emphasis on evangelism, personal devotion, Methodist mores [or Wesleyan disciplines], and openness in expressing one's evangelical commitment.[7]

And that is true. But that is not sufficient when key doctrines are at stake or key policies with doctrinal implications are at stake, as we are all facing today. I was on the General Synod of the Church of England for 15

---

[7] George M. Marsden, 'Reformed and American' in David F. Wells, ed., *Reformed Theology in America: A History of its Modern Development* (Grand Rapids: Eerdmans, 1985), 3.

At the same time as
we need to exercise
our minds in more
disciplined thinking, we
need to realise there is a
spiritual war going on.

years, one of the panel of chairmen (for the debates), and eventually on the Standing Committee (now the Archbishops' Council). There I saw, first-hand, too many good evangelicals 'go with the flow' – a liberalising flow. And they still do, especially when they become bishops!

What can you do about it? Many things need to be done about it.

Certainly, there needs be better general theological understanding, but not an 'ivory tower scholasticism'. And in that better understanding, one focus now needs to be on the doctrine of man. The previous great doctrinal crises in the church were, in the fourth and fifth centuries, over the doctrine of God; at the Reformation, over salvation and the church; and today, it is over the doctrine of man.

But at the same time as we need to exercise our minds in more disciplined thinking, we need to realise there is a spiritual war going on. As Paul says:

> For though we walk in the flesh, we are not waging war according to the flesh. For the weapons of our warfare are not of the flesh but have divine power to destroy strongholds. We destroy arguments and every lofty opinion raised against the knowledge of God, and take every thought captive to obey Christ (2 Cor 10:3–5).

How we need to pray for the Holy Spirit to guide and strengthen us!

On Marriage and Sex

So, finally, one very important reason why we need the English Reformed tradition preserved is this. I believe it has been more right on marriage and sex, a fundamental in the doctrine of man, than the tradition of the Westminster Assembly. Three things are to be said.

First, there are the purposes of marriage. The difference between the English Reformers and the Westminster tradition is over the first purpose of marriage. The English Reformed tradition in its marriage service said it was, 'the procreation of children, to be brought up in the fear and nurture of the Lord, and to the praise of his holy Name.' But the Westminster Confession puts it like this in Chapter 24, section 2:

> Marriage was [first] ordained for the mutual help of husband and wife; [only then, secondly] for the increase of mankind with a legitimate issue, and of the church with an holy seed; and [finally] for prevention of uncleanness.

Of course, Genesis 1 comes before Genesis 2. And the first command, the first words, in fact, to man were: 'be fruitful and multiply' (Gen 1:28). That was, indeed, the blessing of God. Many are so sad when they cannot have children. But the words, 'it is not good that the man should

35

be alone; I will make a helper fit for him,' come in Genesis 2:18. Of course, if the number one purpose of marriage is companionship – well, two men or two women can fit the bill, as people have been claiming recently!

Getting this wrong has serious demographic considerations. We are living at time of what *The Times* newspaper calls a 'Demographic apocalypse', for 'collapsing birth rates will turn our world upside down.' For, contrary to general awareness, there is serious underpopulation in much of the world today in spite of the demographic momentum in which longevity masks the fall in birth rate. In China with its one-child policy the consequences have been serious; and other parts of the Far East are even worse. And England and Wales are also failing in this regard. For 2.1 children is the replacement fertility requirement. But in England and Wales the TFR (total fertility rate) in 2020 was 1.68, the lowest since records began. And other European countries are lower. So, in the developed world, we all have to expect consequential adverse economic and social conditions.

As is reported:

> In less than a lifetime, China will be half the nation it is today thanks to a rapid population collapse. Greying states in Europe and across the globe will compete for migrants from a still-growing Africa, while others consider turning back the clock on women's rights in a desperate

attempt to save their dying societies with baby booms.[8]

That is why, among other things, not least Christian obedience, we want to preserve the English Reformed doctrine of marriage where children are a blessing not only to their parents but to the wider world; and that is especially so when children are 'brought up in the fear and nurture of the Lord'.

Secondly, and here we are halfway between Rome and Westminster – this English tradition allowed for nullity and separation but not remarriage. Interestingly, even the Westminster Confession Chapter 24, sections 5–6 on divorce and remarriage were excised by the Puritan English Parliament in 1648 and it was published without them in England. But Scotland kept them and so has the mainstream of the Westminster tradition. Unlike Rome, in the English Reformed tradition, the repentant remarried are admitted to Holy Communion. But much more can and needs to be said about all that.

And, thirdly, on sex and marriage, the English tradition benefits from reading the Apocrypha which Article 6 says, 'the Church doth read for example of life and instruction of manners [modern morals];' but it then adds 'yet doth it not apply them to establish any doctrine.'

---

[8] Hugh Tomlinson, 'Demographic Apocalypse,' *Times*, 22 July 2020, https://www.thetimes.co.uk/article/demographic-apocalypse-collapsing-birth-rates-will-turn-our-world-upside-down-bxpbjrbk0

We need the Apocrypha to know something about the intertestamental period. However, in the opening chapter of the Westminster Confession, section 3 says the books of the Apocrypha are 'no part of the canon ... and of no authority ... nor to be any otherwise approved, or made use of, than other human writings.'

But when you read 1 Maccabees 1:10–15 and 2 Maccabees 4:10–17 you read, significantly, that the Maccabean revolution was occasioned by the Hellenisation of the Jews under Antiochus IV. And the establishment of a Gymnasium in Jerusalem was its flash point.

For Greek Gymnasia shocked even the Romans and so even more the Jews. To quote the French Historian Henri Marrou:

> their [the Romans] sense of modesty was shocked by its nudity, and they regarded homosexuality – which centred round the gymnasium – as something that Greek civilisation should be ashamed of.[9]

However, when the temple was eventually cleansed after its desecration by Antiochus IV – with its abomination of desolation (a pagan altar) – a Festival of Dedication was established. And Jesus was in the temple on one occasion at the time of 'the Feast of Dedication' (John 10:22–23). And everyone would have known about the Gymnasium

---

[9] Henri-Irénée Marrou, *A History of Education in Antiquity*, trans. George Lamb (New York: Sheed & Ward, 1956), 249.

and the paganism from which the Jews had escaped. That escape was what the feast celebrated! So arguments that the New Testament Christ and the Apostles did not know about a homosexual culture, such as we now have, are quite implausible.

We should therefore read the Apocrypha – not for doctrine, but to know the background to the New Testament (there, of course, is an ESV version now of the Apocrypha).

And with that, I rest my case, that the English Reformed tradition, the tradition of Canon A5 – the 'canon of canons' according to the Church of England (Worship and Doctrine) Measure 1974, and spelt out in the Reform Covenant – that tradition is not only different from other Reformed traditions but also is certainly worth preserving. For while no tradition is perfect, of all the Reformed traditions this can claim to be the most Scriptural, *when true to itself*!

Appendix: The Reform Covenant

We who subscribe this Covenant bind ourselves together in fellowship to uphold, defend and spread the gospel of Jesus Christ according to the doctrine of the Church of England.

We affirm the definition of this doctrine that is set out in Canon A5 as follows:

The doctrine of the Church of England is grounded in the Holy Scriptures, and in such teachings of the ancient Fathers and Councils of the Church as are agreeable to the said Scriptures. In particular such doctrine is to be found in the Thirty-Nine Articles of Religion, the *Book of Common Prayer*, and the Ordinal.

Specifically, we lay emphasis on the following:

1. The triune personhood of God as the Father, the Son and the Holy Spirit, and the historical incarnation of the Son of God through the Virgin Mary.

2. The substitutionary sin-bearing death, bodily resurrection, present heavenly reign, and future return to judgement of Jesus Christ the incarnate Son.

3. The universality of sin, the present justification of sinners by grace through faith in Christ alone, and their supernatural regeneration and new life through the Holy Spirit.

4. The calling of the Church and of all Christian people to a life of holiness and prayer according to the Scriptures.

5. The primacy of evangelism and nurture in each local church's task of setting forth the kingdom of God.

6. The significance of personal present repentance and faith as determining eternal destiny.

7. The finality of God's revelation in Jesus Christ and the uniqueness of his ministry as our prophet, priest and king, and the only Saviour of sinners.

8. The infallibility and supreme authority of 'God's Word written' and its clarity and sufficiency for the resolving of disputes about Christian faith and life. (See Article 20).

Our understanding of God's way of life for his people includes:

a. The special teaching responsibility of ordained leaders within the every member ministry of the body of Christ, and the need to provide for its continuance.

b. The unique value of women's ministry in the local congregation but also the divine order of male headship, which makes the headship of women as priests in charge, incumbents, dignitaries and bishops inappropriate.

c. The vital importance of monogamous life-long marriage for the care and nurture of children, and the well being of human society.

d. The rightness of sexual intercourse in heterosexual marriage, and the wrongness of such activity both outside it and in all its homosexual forms.

e. The urgent need for decentralisation at national, diocesan and deanery level, and the need radically to reform the present shape of episcopacy and pastoral discipline, to enable local churches to evangelise more effectively.

Also published by the Latimer Trust:

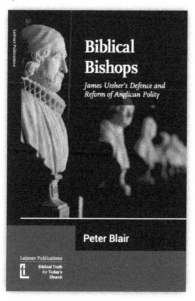

As fissures emerge within the worldwide Anglican communion, the principle and praxis of episcopacy have never been more pertinent. For some Anglicans, bishops are essential for the church. For others, they are something of a necessary evil; baggage from the English reformation that we might be better off without.

These concerns are nothing new. In the seventeenth century, debates surrounding the validity and authority of bishops abounded. Into those debates wrote James Ussher, archbishop of Armagh and Primate of All Ireland. Ussher was a remarkable figure: a preeminent historian, biblical scholar, and theologian, respected by English puritans and Irish Jesuits alike. As is often the case with such luminaries, various camps have claimed Ussher as their own; whether they be puritan, high church, or anglo-catholic.

By studying Ussher's ecclesiastical career and his two works on church government, this study assesses Ussher's episcopalian convictions, particularly regarding the validity and authority of bishops. In doing so, it hopes to reintroduce Ussher to the evangelical Anglican world, and demonstrate that episcopacy is not a necessary evil, but a force for good in the church of God.

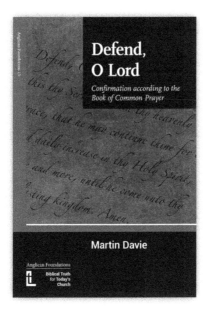

A key way in which the benefits of the work of Christ are conveyed to those who respond to the gospel with repentance and faith is through the two rites of 'Christian initiation': baptism and confirmation. In baptism we die to our old life of sin and death and rise to a new life with God which will be fully revealed at the resurrection of the dead at the end of time.

In confirmation we reaffirm the promises which were made at our baptism, and we are given strength through the Spirit to live the new life we have been given in baptism, and protection from all that would turn us away from God.

The Church of England's normative confirmation service, to which the *Common Worship* services are authorised alternatives, is the confirmation service in the 1662 *Book of Common Prayer*.

This little book provides an introduction to the 1662 service. It describes how confirmation developed in the Early Church and during the Middle Ages and how the Prayer Book confirmation service developed after the Reformation. It also provides a detailed commentary on the Prayer Book service, and answers the ten key questions people today generally ask about confirmation.

In the St Antholin Lecture Series:

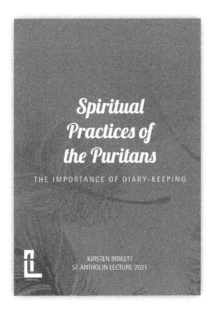

The Puritans wished to live godly lives in heart and thought as well as action. One of the tools they utilised in training their hearts and minds was the practice of diary-writing. In this short overview we see the theory of Puritan diary-writing as worked out by John Beadle, and the inspiring example of the sixteenth-century Puritan Richard Rogers writing about his life.

Future releases:

Bishops Past, Present and Future: A Concise Study summarises the key points of the argument of Martin's major study *Bishops Past, Present and Future* (Gilead Books 2022). It is designed to meet the needs of those who would like to know about the role and importance of bishops in the Church of England, but who would baulk at tackling the 800+ pages of the original book.

This concise study is published in the hope that it will help many in the Church of England, both ordained and lay, to think in a more informed fashion about how bishops should respond to the challenges facing the Church of England at this critical point in its history as it considers how to move forward following the publication of the Living in Love and Faith material.

Lightning Source UK Ltd.
Milton Keynes UK
UKHW010621300922
409658UK00004B/1137

9 781906 327767